A Brief Histor

G000089760

A Brief History of Birmingham

Peter Leather

to the people of Birmingham, my adopted home

BREWIN
BOOKS

First Published by
Brewin Books Ltd, Studley, Warwickshire.
in March 2001

ISBN1 85858 187 7

British Library Cataloguing in Publication

A catalogue record for this book is available
from the British Library

Typeset in Times New Roman and
made and printed in Great Britain by
Supaprint (Redditch) Ltd
Redditch, Worcestershire.
Website: www.supaprint.com
E-mail: admin@supaprint.com

Acknowledgements

Birmingham has been blessed with many great historians, from William Hutton to Carl Chinn, and this book owes a debt to all of them. It was Victor Skipp whose books first introduced me to Birmingham history but I have also learned much from the words, written and spoken, of John Aitken, Patrick Baird, Steve Bassett, Asa Briggs, Carl Chinn, George Demidowicz, Robert Dent, Margaret Gelling, Conrad Gill, Mike Hodder, Eric Hopkins, Richard Holt, Chris Upton and Sarah Wager, a number of whom I have the pleasure of knowing personally. I owe much too to the many individual researchers who have added something to my knowledge; and the hundreds of students who have attended my talks and courses, and helped me to correct and refine my ideas. Finally I'd like to thank two publishers: Alan Brewin, of course, for producing this book and supporting my wish to keep the price as low as possible; and Ross Crawford, editor of *Birmingham MetroNews*, whose printing of my columns all these years has helped sustain my research into this wonderful city.

Introduction

My own bit of Birmingham history started in 1984 when I arrived here via Liverpool, London and Oxford. The reason I came was simple - it was in the middle! Like so many others before me, I fell in love with the place and now consider myself, above all else, an adopted Brummie.

In those first few years, unemployed and with time on my hands, I really got to know the area, roaming about on foot or using my £3.50 a fortnight West Midlands Off-Peak Travel Pass.

Having dabbled for a while with fiction-writing, I saw a chance to make a bit of money writing travel articles for newspapers and magazines. In 1988 I approached the *Daily News* (the free newspaper that started up the same year I arrived in Brum) with the idea of a weekly column looking at local historic sites. It was called *Out and About* and gave me my first chance to start researching Birmingham's history and, better still, tell everyone about it!

The *Daily News* became *MetroNews* in 1991 and the following year *Out and About* evolved into *Hidden City* (in circumstances for which I owe a great debt of gratitude to Carl Chinn). It's still going strong last time I looked - you may well have read about this book in there!

Also in 1991, I finally felt confident enough to offer my services as a part-time tutor on Birmingham history to the *University of Birmingham School of Continuing Studies*, (since renamed the *School for Professional and Continuing Education)* where I am now *Lecturer in Birmingham Studies*. My first task, ironically enough, was to give a fifteen-minute talk on William Hutton, Birmingham's first historian, who was also an "immigrant"!

In September that year, I began my first course, grandly named *Rewriting the History of Birmingham*. By way of class notes, I wrote eight *Chapters of Birmingham History* - and that's where this book really started. The original intention was to revise the "chapters" every time the course ran but that never quite happened, and it was only the creation of a new *Birmingham History* course in 1998 that finally made a complete rewrite essential. The eight chapters were expanded into twelve, and *A Brief History of Birmingham* was born.

Birmingham History is part of a two-year *Certificate of Higher Education in Birmingham Studies*, equivalent to the first year of an undergraduate degree. It's good to see the study of our city finally being accepted as a serious academic pursuit.

It's also good to be able to offer my own bite-size version of Birmingham history to the people of a city that has made me so welcome. In my wildest imaginings I hope it may be small enough and cheap enough to find its way into every home and school - ridiculously ambitious, I know, but isn't that what being a Brummie is all about?

Contents

Birmingham Before Birmingham

Landscape and topography dictated the form of early human settlement in the Birmingham area - it is only comparatively recently that we have come to dominate our surroundings rather than them dominating us.

One of the key facts to bear in mind is that Birmingham is about as far from the sea as you can get in England - the hills to the south-west represent a national watershed, feeding both Severn and Trent, and ultimately Bristol Channel and North Sea. So any process of trade or migration or cultural change would take a long time to get here.

Topographical features which today are largely hidden beneath the concrete and tarmac of the city played a decisive role in the region's early development.

Principal among these is the sandstone ridge crossing the city from south-west to north-east via Northfield, Selly Oak, Edgbaston, the city centre, Aston, Erdington and Sutton Coldfield. This is the sort of lightly-soiled ridgeway route that was particularly attractive to early settlers. Clay soils to the east were more fertile but much heavier to cultivate; the pebble beds to the west supported rough heath-land that had little value for farming but was good grazing land. All three were to play their part in Birmingham's early and mediaeval development.

The sandstone ridgeway remained the area's chief through-route in the Roman period and also in the Middle Ages (when it is the only local road shown on the 14th century "Gough" Map). Even today, the A38, as it has become, is treated as the primary cross-city route by road traffic planners.

The route is not without its obstacles, principally the Tame Valley that cuts deeply through the sandstone, creating the cliffs that once existed at Salford. A succession of fords and bridges marked an important crossing point at Perry Barr.

The ridgeway passes a little to the west of the crossing point of the Rea at Digbeth/Deritend that became the focus of mediaeval Birmingham - it is not clear what if any importance this location had prior to the market developments of the 12th century.

The earliest evidence for human settlement in the Birmingham area is provided by finds of Lower Palaeolithic stone tools - these are hard to date but could be tens or even hundreds of thousands of years old. They would have been made by tribes of hunters passing through the area in between the Ice Ages.

Hunter-gatherers of the Mesolithic period (c.10,000-4,000BC) are well attested by finds in the Sandwell Valley, and it would be fair to presume, backed up by similar finds from Oscott, that they ventured farther down the Tame too.

From this time on there has probably always been a human presence in the Birmingham area, but it is likely that the region was treated as a marginal one on the edge of territories primarily based in the Severn, Trent and Avon Valleys - this certainly seems to be the case in the Late Iron Age/Roman period at the dawn of recorded history, when three tribal territories meet here.

Birmingham should not therefore be seen as central to anything that was happening in this period but rather as an area into which neighbouring tribes might expand in times of prosperity and population growth.

One such phase happened during the Bronze Age (2,400-700BC), a time when marginal territories all over Britain, from the Yorkshire Moors to the Highlands of Scotland were first being settled. Birmingham's oldest surviving man-made structure, the Kingstanding burial mound, may date from the very start of this period or the end of the preceding Neolithic (4,000-2,400 BC). There is another likely burial mound and records of a wooden trackway in Sutton Park.

Far more numerous are the "Burnt Mounds" dating from the late 2nd millennium BC that are found alongside the city's streams and rivers. Consisting of heat-cracked pebbles and datable charcoal, they may have been used for cooking or sauna-style bathing - but they clearly point to intensified human presence. Their study by Birmingham archaeologists including Mike Hodder (who strongly supports the "sauna" interpretation) have made them internationally known among specialists.

If there was indeed a "Bronze Age boom" it soon came to an end, possibly due to climatic changes. The subsequent Iron Age (700BC-43AD) has left little trace in the city with the principal settlement sites, now represented by heavily defended "Hillforts", once more grouping around the Severn, Trent and Avon Valleys.

The prehistoric burial mound at Kingstanding, dating from around 2500 BC, is the oldest known man-made structure in the city

When the Romans invaded Britain in 43AD they found a number of large tribal units which they adapted into their preferred form of local government - the "civitas" or city-state. As before, the Birmingham area was marginal to the principal tribal territories - the Dobunni (centred on Cirencester) to the south-west, the Cornovii (Wroxeter) to the north-west and Corieltauvi (Leicester) to the north-east - and it is not even possible to say to which it belonged.

However, in the early years of the Conquest, a Roman fort was established at Metchley and this became the focus of a network of Roman Roads. Excavations at the fort suggest that it was occupied, in one form or another, for around 150 years. Traces have also been found of a short-lived civilian settlement outside the fort, but there is no evidence as yet of a Roman town developing on or near the site as happened elsewhere.

Elsewhere in the city, the Roman period is represented by two pottery kilns, small settlement sites at Parsons Hill and Castle Bromwich and field patterns in the area east of Sutton Coldfield. But this may not be all - the surprise discovery of an important Roman temple site at Coleshill (which may have some bearing on the question of where the tribal boundaries lay) demonstrates that the history of ancient Birmingham must be treated as strictly provisional.

The Roman Fort of Metchley, occupied between the mid 1st and late 2nd centuries AD, lies buried beneath the University and QE Medical Centre

From Birth to Doom

The birth of Birmingham took place in a time so devoid of historical light that it has been termed "the Dark Ages". No documentary source refers to Birmingham before the Domesday Book of 1086. Archaeological traces of the period at Weoley Castle and Castle Bromwich are enigmatic to say the least.

However, a combination of new historical ideas, reinterpretation of the few available sources, and developments in the study of the meaning and chronology of place-names has cast some light in the darkness, albeit in a highly theoretical way.

The surprising conclusion of all this work is to suggest, contrary to the old established view, that: a) Birmingham did not originate as an Anglo-Saxon village around the Bull Ring; and b) despite the clear evidence that Birmingham was an "insignificant agricultural settlement" (Holt) at the time of the Norman Conquest, it may have had an earlier flowering in the Anglo-Saxon period.

The first thing to consider is the name itself. Birmingham is generally now believed to mean "the *ham* (home) of the *Beormingas* (people of Beorma)". Names of this sort are believed to be both early (6th-7th century) and historically significant, since they refer to the family/tribal groupings of early Anglo-Saxon settlers. No other name in the area has this sort of antiquity or status.

The *Beormingas* may have been part of the westward movement of Anglo-Saxon peoples from East Anglia in the 6th century which led ultimately (in 585?) to the foundation of the Kingdom of Mercia, whose Royal family were the *Iclingas* (people of Icel). Mercia means "Marchland" (ie. borderland) but there is dispute as to whether the "border" is between Anglo-Saxons and Celts, or rival Anglo-Saxon kingdoms.

5

What's in a Name? The derivation of the name "Birmingham" may imply that the site was more important in the Anglo-Saxon period than was once thought

It is no longer believed that the pre-existing British population was driven out or annihilated by the Anglo-Saxons, but rather that the two peoples merged under Anglo-Saxon leadership. Penda (King of Mercia 626-655?) is now seen as an ally rather than opponent of the princes of Powys at the battle of Caer Luitcoed (Wall/Lichfield).

The Lichfield area provides evidence for the survival of British speakers into the 7th century as the change from Celtic *Letoceto* to Welsh *Luitcoed* could not have happened earlier. It has also been suggested that the Anglo-Saxon diocese of Lichfield (founded by St Chad c.670) had a Celtic predecessor.

Place-names in the Birmingham area as elsewhere show survival of Celtic names for topographical features such as the rivers (Tame and Cole) and hills (Barr). The River Tame linked Birmingham to the Mercian royal seat at Tamworth. George Demidowicz believes that the name Cole ("hazel") once had a wider significance since it was also the name of the river we now call Rea (Anglo-Saxon for "river") – he suggests it may have been the Celtic name of the area through which the two rivers ran.

The territory of the *Beormingas* was initially the southernmost extent of Mercia but it is no longer thought correct to see this (as Skipp 1980 did) as a boundary between Anglian Mercians and Saxon *Hwicce* (the people who later formed Worcestershire). Recent work suggests that the *Hwicce* too were originally Anglian, coming from the east, and only subsequently merged with the Saxons as they spread up the Severn.

Whatever the case, the territory was clearly marginal and therefore vulnerable to sub-division - which would explain how it could have shrunk so much by Domesday. Evidence of this process is provided by charters granting valuable woodland resources in Kings Norton and Yardley to landholders elsewhere.

An attempt was first made to reconstruct the Birmingham territory by Sarah Wager in a 1988 University of Birmingham MPhil thesis, applying the bold and contentious new theories of her tutor, Steven Bassett - her conclusions are summarised and developed in Bassett's "Anglo-Saxon Birmingham" (see reading list).

Bassett argues that it is possible to reconstruct ancient "land-units" by tracing them back through time from the Middle Ages. This is particularly the case with Mediaeval parishes, which can in many cases be shown to be subdivisions of larger Anglo-Saxon *parochiae*, themselves deriving from earlier estates.

The theory has been most successfully applied to the area around Wootton Wawen with its Anglo-Saxon church. Eleven adjoining mediaeval parishes can be shown to be "chapels" of Wootton Wawen and thus all part of one big Anglo-Saxon parish. Furthermore, an early 8th century charter names the area from which the parish evolved as the territory of the *Stoppingas*, another Anglo-Saxon tribal grouping.

Sarah Wager attempted to do the same for Birmingham. She found that a number of mediaeval churches in the city had links with each other that seemed to predate the establishment of county boundaries in the 10th or 11th century, eg. Aston with Yardley (Warwickshire/Worcestershire), Aston with Handsworth (Warwickshire/Staffordshire), and Harborne with Edgbaston (Staffordshire/Warwickshire). On the basis of this and other evidence she proposed an original Birmingham territory stretching west-east from West Bromwich to Castle Bromwich and north-south from the borders of Sutton (whose name implies northern affiliations) to the borders of Kings Norton and Northfield (northern outposts of Bromsgrove?).

Wager's presumed territory would have been controlled from Birmingham and catered for spiritually by a minster church at either Aston or Harborne (favoured by Bassett), both of which have the early name of St Peter's. But where was Birmingham?

The current view, as explained in the next chapter, is that the Bull Ring area was only developed in the 12th century, and that Anglo-Saxon Birmingham should be sought elsewhere. Wager's solution is that it must be west of Aston ("east-town") or the name doesn't make sense - she suggests the Hockley area where the Roman Road crossed the Brook. There are two other possibilities: 1) that New Street (which is certainly no newer than the 14th century) was the link between old Birmingham and the new 12th century town, thus placing the old site in the Broad Street area; or 2) that it was based around the old Parsonage Moat – now buried beneath the Arcadian Centre – with Dudley Street and Pinfold Street the original road in from the west. In either case, there would seem to be little chance of ever finding Anglo-Saxon Birmingham.

When New Street was "new" it may have provided a link between Anglo-Saxon Birmingham and the new 12th century market town around the Bull Ring

Mediaeval Birmingham

Whether it is true or not that Birmingham started life as the centre of an Anglo-Saxon family/tribal territory, it is certainly the case that it emerges into recorded history in the Domesday Book of 1086 as an "insignificant agricultural settlement" (Holt).

The Domesday figures, however unreliable and hard to interpret, show Birmingham as one of the poorest manors in a generally poor area. The rental value of £1 is one fifth of that for Aston and Northfield, which themselves pale into insignificance beside a South Warwickshire manor such as Brailes, valued at £55.

Once more the Birmingham area appears marginal in a county whose population and farming activity can be seen to diminish from south to north with the bulk concentrated in the Feldon of South Warwickshire and the Avon Valley.

It used to be thought that the process whereby Birmingham grew from a tiny backwater village to a major market centre was a gradual one, but the transformation is now believed to have been far more dramatic and sudden, and one of Birmingham's own making. It was not, in the opinion of recent historians, any great natural advantages possessed by the Rea crossing at Digbeth/Deritend that made it the focus of a regional road network but rather the deliberate implanting of a new market at the Bull Ring. It could be argued that Aston is more favourably located as a market centre and that it was not nature but personal acumen that swung the balance.

In this light the Market Charter of 1166 becomes a priceless historic document. The fact that the location of the market changes from the Lord of the Manor's "castle" (ie. moated manor house) in the original grant to his "town" in the confirmation of 1189 may mean that a new town based around the Bull Ring was created between these dates. Features of the Birmingham Moat interpreted as dating from the 12th and 13th centuries and finds of reused Norman stonework in St Martin's may support this idea, as do the discoveries from recent archaeological digs in advance of the Bull Ring redevelopment – including the town well and what may be the original town boundary ditch.

The tomb effigy in St Martin's church of one of the mediaeval Lords of Birmingham who helped make the town a thriving market centre

The Lord of the Manor who took this initiative was Peter de Bermingham and it may be that his actions were just as important to the rise of Birmingham as anything that Matthew Boulton and Joseph Chamberlain later did. Birmingham Market was among the earliest in the Midlands, a century ahead of rivals such as Sutton Coldfield and Solihull, and thus with a great advantage in terms of profiting from the population expansion and economic growth of the times. A belated attempt by Aston to set up a rival market at Deritend proved futile and the street was absorbed into Birmingham.

Peter is also credited with the creation of the Borough of Birmingham and its counter-part the Foreign, a division lasting down to the 19th century between the built-up part and the open lands to the west, including the Lord of the Manor's private hunting estate at Rotton Park (first recorded 1307).

His actions made Birmingham a centre of attraction for ambitious people from the increasingly over-populated agricultural manors of Warwickshire and Worcestershire who wished to rid themselves of feudal ties by becoming free rent-paying burgesses. One such was John of Studley who, in 1250, becomes the first historically recorded Brummie.

By this time Birmingham's market had been supplemented by the grant of an Ascensiontide Fair, which may tie in with the town's growing importance in the Welsh cattle trade. Virtually nothing is known about this potentially vital part of the local economy but suffice to say that the agriculturally poor heathlands to the west may finally have come into their own as grazing land. It has certainly been demonstrated by recent archaeological digs that Birmingham had a major leather industry from at least the 14th century, with large tanning pits off Edgbaston Street.

The burgesses of Birmingham also dabbled in the cloth trade (but on an absolutely tiny scale compared with Coventry) and serviced local agriculture through the production of farming implements and horse-fittings. Their homes occupied the burgage plots laid out in the 12th century and later - Skipp (1980) claimed to have identified 75 such plots on later maps. Two burgesses represented Birmingham in the Parliament of 1275 - a further sign of importance.

Growth in the 13th century, a boom time nationally, allowed the Lords of the Manor to endow a Priory/Hospital of St Thomas (first recorded 1286) and rebuild St Martin's on a grander scale towards the end of the century. The size of the town at this time is demonstrated by the fact that a conflagration which took place sometime between 1281 and 1313 was known as the "Great Fire of Birmingham".

A chance reference to "Birmingham Pieces" (believed to be some sort of precious metal objects) in a document of 1308 signals a distant ancestor of the town's jewellery trade.

The year 1327 provides a useful point of reference for assessing how far Birmingham had come since 1086. Tax returns show the town third in Warwickshire, fast overtaking Warwick itself and only really lagging behind Coventry, which was then one of the top five towns in England. Also that year, Lord William de Bermingham was summoned to Parliament - but sadly for him at a time before this carried with it an hereditary peerage.

The mediaeval Priory/Hospital of St Thomas has left no trace but is commemorated on this plaque in Old Square

The rest of the century was a time of national crisis with famine and the Black Death, but Birmingham was strong enough to ride out the storm as local agriculture and rival market towns collapsed. The survivors benefited from there being more to go around, and great fortunes and landed estates were built.

The "Gild of the Holy Cross", founded as a religious institution in 1392, became a meeting place for the town's elite whose leader, the Gild Master ranked higher than the High Bailiff. It controlled the all important bridges over the Rea.

Remarkably little can be said about 15th century Birmingham - it was the age of the Wars of the Roses but the de Berminghams managed to keep out of trouble. For the most part the processes of recovery begun after the Black Death continued with more and more wealth being concentrated into fewer and fewer hands. Birmingham next enters the glare of history at the time of the Reformation.

Tudor and Stuart Birmingham

The 16th and 17th centuries were times of great change and still greater progress: Birmingham was transformed from an essentially agricultural market centre whose "industries" (tanning, cloth-making, smithing) were all farming-related, to a burgeoning industrial centre almost ready to export to the world. The absence of industrial raw materials in Birmingham was to be no more of a hindrance than the dearth of good agricultural land had been.

The two principal institutions of mediaeval Birmingham - the hereditary manorial family and the Catholic church - came to an end, by coincidence, in the same decade - the 1530s. The last of the de Bermingham lords, Edward, was forced to cede his estates to the Crown in 1536 after being accused of highway robbery and imprisoned in the Tower of London. The story goes that he was "set up" by his Dudley overlords, desperate for money and greedy to get their hands on the gold-mine of Birmingham's market. The estates did finally go to Dudley in 1545, in the shape of the immensely powerful John Dudley, Viscount Lisle, who became Earl of Warwick in 1547 and Duke of Northumberland from 1551, and was virtual ruler of England during the reign of boy-king, Edward VI.

Gill speculates that, far from being damaged by this turn of events, Birmingham may actually have received a boost from its businesslike new master. In any case, his lordship was short-lived, ending with downfall and execution after the failed attempt to set Lady Jane Grey on the throne in 1553.

Birmingham was returned to the Crown but only until 1555 when the manor was sold to Thomas Marrow, whose family held the lordship until the 18th century. But this was a very different sort of ownership from that of the mediaeval de Berminghams.

Also in 1536, the Reformation came to Birmingham. Henry VIII had taken control of the English church by the Act of Supremacy of 1534 and now his chief minister, Thomas Cromwell was about to embark on what we might today call "asset-stripping" in the form of the Dissolution of the Monasteries. Some 800 religious houses were seized by the Crown between 1536 and 1540 to be sold off at a great profit. Among them was the tiny Priory/Hospital of St Thomas.

The fate of the buildings is not so important as that of the Priory's extensive lands. They were ideal investments for the town's rising merchant elite, and many great Birmingham landowners of later centuries got their start then, including Vesey, Colmore, Phillips and Smallbrook.

Traditionally dated to 1368, the Old Crown is now thought to have been built around 1500 as the Gild House of St John's Deritend, a chapel of Aston

With the monasteries all sold off, governmental eyes turned to the gilds and chantry endowments. The first commissioners sent to

Birmingham in 1545 reported that social services were good and that the chantry priests led a useful existence. But by 1547 a harder line was taken and all were dissolved regardless. This finished off the Gild of the Holy Cross in New Street but didn't affect the recently established Lench Trust, which covered much the same ground but without the religious connotations. It might be wondered if the allocation of road and bridge maintenance (a traditional concern of the Gild) to the Trust in 1540 was done with some degree of foresight. Some of the Gild's assets were returned to allow the founding of King Edward's Free Grammar School in 1552.

A more welcome visitor to Birmingham in the 1530s was John Leland, who wrote his famous account of the town. Despite his insistence on the predominance of smiths, there were also at that time still plenty of leather-workers and a few cloth-makers. The cattle market was prospering: the name "Bull Ring" first appears c.1550, when the old open space was fast filling up with "The Shambles" of butchers' shops. The continued importance of the Welsh trade is demonstrated by the presence in the town centre of a Welsh Market, a Welsh Cross and a Welsh End. Leather was still a big enough local commodity in the early 17th century for inspectors to be appointed and the old market tollhouse to be renamed the Leather Hall.

But it was already clear that the future lay in metal. The farm-implement trade developed into more specialised blade-making including cutlery and weapons. Already in 1513-14 Birmingham had supplied a large order of horse-fittings and weapons to the King. As technology changed in the 17th century, blades gave way to guns.

The biggest technological advance of the 16th century was the development of the blast furnace for smelting iron. Now at last the vast mineral wealth of the Black Country could be exploited - and Birmingham was to be the marketing centre. As timber supplies in the Black Country began to be exhausted, manufacture moved down the Tame Valley with a bloomery in the woods of Perry by

1538, a hammer-mill in Handsworth in the 1540s and an iron furnace on the Holbrook by 1591. Later came Bromford Forge in 1605 and Aston Furnace in 1615.

Birmingham had its next big brush with national history in the English Civil War. As with so many other manufacturing towns, it sided with Parliament, although there was a strong Royalist element among the town's poor. Local landowners too, such as Thomas Holte of newly built Aston Hall, might forget their mercantile origins and stand by the King. Holte went one better: as Charles marched south in October 1642, having addressed his troops at Kingstanding, he stayed overnight at Aston Hall. The people of Birmingham were less hospitable and robbed his baggage train as he marched through.

The town paid the price for this insult the following year when it was sacked by Prince Rupert on April 3. Much of the then timber-framed Moor Street/Dale End area was fired. Strategically this so-called Battle of Birmingham was no more than a skirmish but it proved a major propaganda coup for the Parliamentarian cause.

Birmingham recovered from the ravages of war more rapidly than already declining Coventry and finally overtook its great rival. Rapid population growth in the last quarter of the century was aided by immigration. The ever-expanding iron industry was now joined by copper and brass. The "Toyshop of Europe" was just around the corner.

Mural in Colmore Circus depicting the events of the Civil War "Battle of Birmingham" in April 1643

Hutton's Birmingham

The 18th century is the age of William Hutton, Birmingham's first historian. As a historian he has many faults, and much of what he has to say about Birmingham's earlier history must be treated with extreme caution (even though, in fairness to him, he did take the trouble to visit "antiquities" in person); but his "eye-witness" account of the town in the second half of the century, although full of idiosyncrasies, remains a priceless record.

What Hutton witnessed was the dramatic expansion of a town already thriving at the time of his birth in 1723 to something eight times larger when he died in 1815. In population terms the leap was from around 12,000 to near 100,000. He counted only fifteen streets that dated back to the 1650s or earlier compared with fifty in 1731, and that was just the beginning.

William Hutton first came to Birmingham as a penniless runaway in 1741 but was eventually to write the first History of Birmingham in 1780

In 1700 the built-up area of the town remained relatively small and confined, still based largely around the mediaeval core. The first new development took place on the land between Edgbaston Street and New Street, which was later to become the notorious Froggery slum district.

Next came the acquisition by gift of "Mr Phillips barley close" for the building of a much needed new church to take some of the load off St Martin's. The choice of name had more to do with this world than the next! This was the first of many subdivisions of the mediaeval parish.

The area around St Philip's, consecrated in 1715, became one of the most desirable residential districts in the town, vying with another development, The Square (later Old Square), built in 1713 on the former priory site, which had been owned by the Holtes and the Smallbrooks in turn before being acquired by Quaker iron-monger, John Pemberton in 1697.

The development of the "green belt" of former priory and manorial lands surrounding the urban core is the key factor in Birmingham's 18th century growth. The best known example is the Colmore estate, the northern part of which later became the Jewellery Quarter. This fact, together with the survival of the estate's central feature, St Paul's Square has led to continued interest in its history. Licensed by Act of Parliament in 1746, building started at the Colmore Row end and progressed north-west. Edmund Street was early, Great Charles and Lionel Streets somewhat later. Development reached St Paul's Square in the 1770s and 80s. Houses were built as residences with gardens but such was the pressure of industrial expansion that they were rapidly taken over by manufacturers and the gardens in-filled with workshops.

The same thing happened on the adjacent Weaman estate, clustered around its church, St Mary's, opened in 1774. Here it was the gun trade that moved in, creating the Gun Quarter. On the other side of town was the Jennens estate with its chapel of St Bartholomew (1749), the oldest of the three.

Georgian architecture encircled the town from Easy Row to Moor Street, making a developmental "growth-ring" which is all the easier to read due to the lack of any major topographical obstacle to uniform growth - but it also spelled the doom of a lot of Birmingham's 18th century heritage when the Inner Ring Road occupied much of the same ground in the 1960s.

The Georgian elegance of St Paul's Square is a rare
survival of the 18th century growth of Birmingham as it
finally spread beyond its mediaeval bounds

Beyond the "ring", significant development focused on the old manorial lands in Digbeth, acquired by Dr Sherlock from the Marrow family in 1730 and then by Sir Thomas Gooch in 1766, and the Bradford estate in Deritend. This latter proved harder to sell than the others, and the developer was forced to lower prices and offer inducements - perhaps this was due to difficult communications links with the town centre or it was simply a sign that this first great building boom was slowing down.

The French Revolution of 1789 and subsequent wars created an economic crisis and put an end to building projects. Ambitious plans for a grand Georgian crescent off Broad Street were left uncompleted.

As the central area filled up, new residential suburbs appeared and were just as rapidly engulfed by the town. Hutton's list of select suburbs comprises Sand Pits, Bath Row, Islington (Broad Street) and New Town Row, to which could be added Ashted (1788) and Summer Hill (1790).

Those who grew rich from Birmingham industry but no longer wished to live amid it were forced to go farther and farther afield. "Country" houses, some owned by old money, others by the nouveau riche, sprang up in the still rural surroundings of places such as Sparkbrook, Moseley and Washwood Heath.

Despite its size, the town lacked any real municipal government and still relied on the old parish officers. Hutton believed that not being an incorporated borough had been positively beneficial to growth as it allowed go-ahead non-conformists (such as himself!) to settle there. This oft-repeated view is now disputed.

Some of the institutions essential to a large town gradually began to emerge: a prison in Pinfold Street (1733), a workhouse in Lichfield Street (1734), a Court of Requests for the settlement of small debts (1752), and the first General Hospital (1779). There were also Birmingham's first newspaper, Aris's Gazette (1741), the Theatre Royal in New Street (1774) and the first subscription library (1779). The Improvement Acts of 1769 and later put responsibility for up-keep of streets and public places in the hands of the Street Commissioners, who provided Birmingham's first municipal building, the Public Office on Moor Street (where the old Moor Street Station now stands), in 1807.

The Priestley Riots of 1791 showed that tensions did exist between the non-conformist free-thinkers who played such a leading role in the town and the masses of the population but generally social relations were good - and this was to be vitally important as Birmingham found its political voice in the early 19th century.

Industrial Birmingham 1 - Manufacture

The classic "Industrial Revolution" image of "dark satanic mills" created by great leaps in technology is no longer seen as true of Birmingham. Eric Hopkins argues that, not only was the 18th century industrial development of Birmingham far different from this, but it was the Northern cities that were atypical and Birmingham the norm.

To Hopkins, what happened in Birmingham was not so much a revolution as an explosion primed long in advance. Victor Skipp (1979) traces the origins of local industry all the way back to the dawn of time: "If a beneficent Creator had laid out a geological palette specifically so that man could 'bring forth' the Industrial Revolution, he could hardly have done better than 'geological accident' did in the Black Country. Everything required was there ... and all within the space of a few miles - not just the coal, but the ironstone, and the limestone, so essential as a flux in the smelting process; not just the fireclay but the moulding sand ... and Etruria Marl ... so useful for making tough engineering bricks; even the 'Rowley Rag' ... and the Lickey quartzite for the making of road metal and the foundation of railway tracks. The industrial 'blast-off' could hardly have taken place from any other launching pad".

As already mentioned in "Tudor and Stuart Birmingham", the development of the blast furnace in the 16th century led to a considerable expansion of Black Country iron-making which spread down the Tame Valley into the Birmingham area in the late 16th and early 17th century. Also in the 17th century, Birmingham water-mills, which were already being used for blade-making, began to be converted to the more truly industrial tasks of rolling and slitting metal. The unifying factor in all this is water-power, at that time the only means of driving machinery other than brute strength.

So it was that when button-manufacturer, Matthew Boulton decided to leave the town centre for pastures new in 1760, he sought a water-mill that could power his new manufactory. Possibly disappointed by the Cole at Sarehole Mill, he headed north to Soho on Hockley Brook. Over the next few years he developed a complex of workshops employing up to a thousand people - but it was not a factory in the northern sense but instead a bringing together of many individual craftsmen under the same roof.

Soho House, home of Matthew Boulton and now a museum reflecting the leading role played by Birmingham in the "Industrial Revolution"

Boulton was not the first to do this. John Taylor had a large button manufactory in Dale End in the 1750s. Increasingly since the Civil War, Birmingham's metal-working skills had been focused on small items, known at the time as "toys", of which buttons and buckles were the two most important. Demand for iron had already grown sufficiently by the early 18th century for the raw material to be imported from as far afield as Russia. Soon it was followed by brass, at first brought in ready-made but worked in the town from the 1740s and massively expanding after the breaking of the copper monopoly by the Birmingham Metal Company in 1781.

Boulton soon found water-power insufficient and unreliable for Soho, which had rapidly become a major tourist attraction, visited by many European ambassadors and crowned heads. In 1775 he began his epoch-making partnership with James Watt, who had not actually invented the steam engine but made it commercially viable. Boulton's initial interest in Watt's invention was solely as a power-source for Soho, but he soon recognised its saleability. At first constructed under contract, production of Watt's patented pumping engine and later his rotary engine (1781) was finally based at the new Soho Foundry in 1796.

There was another creative genius connected with Soho - William Murdock - but his breakthroughs in gas and locomotive technology were not followed up, possibly due to lack of money, possibly jealousy on the part of Watt. The use at Soho in 1802 of the first two gas-lamps ever to appear in public did not lead to anything further and the industry was developed elsewhere. The 1822 Gas Retort House discovered in Gas Street in the early 1990s and believed to be the oldest surviving one in the world has only an indirect link back to Murdock.

The great irony is that the steam engine, that most famous of all Birmingham inventions, was of little use in the town until well into the 19th century. Although Birmingham had more patents to its name by 1800 than anywhere else, they were mostly to do with making the better button. As Hopkins points out, the inventions which Birmingham needed for its craft based industries - stamp, press, lathe and draw-bench - had been made long before.

Typical of the Birmingham penchant for small, good quality, easily exportable items was the jewellery trade. There had been jewellers in Birmingham since at least the 14th century but the business really took off in the late 18th. Boulton played his part here too, helping to get the town its own Assay Office in 1773, so that precious metal goods no longer needed to be sent to London for hallmarking. At the same time the previously diffuse trade began to congregate in the hitherto residential quarter of the Colmore estate. There was further expansion in the early 19th century (possibly due to the collapse of the buckle trade and transfer of skills to jewellery making) and still more following the gold rushes of the 1840s-50s. Just as the jewellers congregated on the Colmore estate, so did gun-makers on the Weaman estate. Gun-making went back to the Civil War period and really took off with a big government order in the 1690s. This trade too relied on division of labour into many different stages of production - in the 1860s there were thirty-two types of "material men" and sixteen of "setters-up".

So why Birmingham? Hopkins concludes, "The growth of trade, the improvement in transport facilities, the beginning of professional banking, the growth of population and the development of the Black Country iron industry all took effect on a vigorous local economy which was already developing fast by 1750".

It may not look much but this is quite possibly the oldest surviving gasworks in the world - the 1822 Gas Retort House in Gas Street

Industrial Birmingham 2 - Transport

A manufacturing town, no matter how creative and hard-working, cannot function unless it has means of getting its products to its customers. Birmingham, as the most land-locked town in England, had a considerable problem in that respect.

In the Middle Ages, as Birmingham's role as a regional market grew, a network of roads evolved around the town connecting it to all the other main centres in the Central Midlands. But only the road passing through the town between Bromsgrove and Lichfield (the present A38) was seen as nationally important.

With the massive expansion of trade in the later 17th and 18th centuries, pressure on the road network grew both in terms of personal travel and goods transport. The country's first recorded time-tabled coach service ran between Birmingham and Chester (for boats to Ireland) in 1637. Later in the century and particularly in the early 1700s the transportation of raw materials by cart and pack-horse became a major factor in Birmingham's burgeoning industrial growth.

All this proved too much for what were in essence still mediaeval lanes - the belt of clay-lands east of the town was a particular obstacle to trade, virtually impassable at certain times of the year. Responsibility for the upkeep of roads lay with the parish Councils and their elected "surveyors of highways", who had the right to call out all able-bodied men to work on the roads for a number of days each year. Bridges were maintained either by the parish or a local trust - as has already been seen, responsibility for the Rea bridge at Digbeth-Deritend passed from the Gild of the Holy Cross to Lench's Trust in the 16th century.

The desperate need for road improvement led to the introduction of turnpike roads, named after the spiked barrier used to bar traffic, which paid for their own upkeep by charging tolls. The system started up in 1662 but only really took off after the administration was transferred from the local JPs to private trusts in 1707.

Roads in the Birmingham area began to be turnpiked from 1726 and the process continued for a hundred years: Stratford Road 1726, Warwick Road 1726, Bristol Road 1727, Old Walsall Road 1727, Soho Road 1727, Coventry Road 1745, Hagley Road 1753, Washwood Heath Road 1760, Dudley Road 1761, Alcester Road 1767, Lichfield Road 1807, Pershore Road 1825, New Walsall Road 1831.

There were many faults with the turnpike system - some trusts were happy to take the tolls but not so keen to spend money on maintenance, and William Hutton gives a pretty bad impression of the state of the local roads in his time - but road transport did improve, so that the coach-trip to London which took three to four days at the start of the 18th century was down to 15 hours by the end of it.

But no amount of road improvement could cope with the endless loads of coal and iron ore coming from the Black Country - in many places the roads wore down into holloways with steep banks on either side. So when, in the mid 18th century, the dream of creating artificial waterways became a reality with the joining of Trent, Mersey and Severn by the *Staffordshire and Worcestershire* canal, the manufacturers of Birmingham were keen to follow suit.

Between 1767 and 1772 James Brindley, "the father of canals" surveyed and built the *Birmingham Canal* linking the town to the *Staffordshire and Worcestershire*. It had an immediate impact, halving the cost of Black Country coal in the town. Success spawned a whole series of other canals - *Birmingham & Fazeley* (1789*), Worcester & Birmingham* (1791-1815), *Warwick & Birmingham* (1793-1800), *Stratford* (1793-1816) - so that by the end of the century land-locked Birmingham was at the heart of the nation's waterways. The original wharf on Easy Row (site of Alpha Tower) later gave way to Gas Street Basin as the town's main docking point but smaller wharves and basins developed throughout

Gas Street Basin, the focus of a canal network which made land-locked Birmingham the centre of the nation's waterways

the network as new factories and warehouses were attracted to the canal-side. When Birmingham became a city in 1889 it had over thirty miles of canals within its bounds.

Water problems on the *Birmingham Canal*, which had been built as a contour canal to avoid major engineering works, were combated at first by the use of Boulton-Watt pumping engines but a final solution was only reached in the 1820s when Thomas Telford re-cut the canal (the *New Main Line*) and established Rotton Park (now Edgbaston) Reservoir as the system's principal feeder.

Already by this time, proposals were in the air for a new and faster means of transport - the railway - but it was only in 1833 that Birmingham's first two lines were sanctioned - the *London & Birmingham* and the *Grand Junction*, linking to Liverpool and Manchester. The first station to be opened was a temporary halt at Vauxhall (now Duddeston) in 1837 but both lines had termini on Curzon Street by 1839.

Curzon Street Station (1838) is arguably one of the most historically important pieces of railway architecture in the world

As with the canals, the railway network rapidly expanded - *Birmingham & Gloucester* 1840, *Birmingham & Derby* (later *Midland*) 1842 - but competition did not always serve the town's best interests. A power struggle between the *Grand Junction* and the *London & Birmingham*, which eventually led to their merger as the *London & North Western* in 1846 and the opening of New Street Station in 1852-4, encouraged the *Great Western Railway* to set up a rival line and station at Snow Hill (1852). A thwarted attempt to bring all the lines together at a single station (New Street) has left behind a reminder in the shape of the never-completed Duddeston Viaduct.

At first the railways concentrated on long distance traffic and there were few intermediate stops but later in the century suburban lines for the newly invented "commuter" began to develop - *Sutton Coldfield* 1862, *Harborne* 1874, *Birmingham West Suburban* 1876, *North Warwickshire* 1907.

The effect of the railways was just as dramatic as that of the canals. Reduction of the journey time to London by half to under five hours soon wiped out the coach trade, while rail's capacity for handling freight threatened the waterways. However, since many of the canals were now owned or part-owned by railway companies, they remained in use and were only finally done away with, ironically enough, by a return to road haulage in the 20th century.

Birmingham's Government
from Bailiffs to Borough

Birmingham entered the 19th century as a major industrial centre with a population of around 70,000 - but with no proper parliamentary representation and a system of local government which was still essentially that of a mediaeval village.

Although it is now presumed that the development of the borough of Birmingham dates back to Peter de Bermingham and the Market Charter of 1166, there is no evidence that the rights of local burgesses took any written form. The attendance of two Birmingham men at the Burgesses' Parliament of 1275 does not imply that the town was a chartered borough, any more than does the use of the words "Borough" and "Foreign" for the divisions of the Manor from at least the 13th century.

The manorial records which could definitively answer the question were lost in the 18th century, but even if Birmingham had been a chartered borough at some stage in the Middle Ages (which seems unlikely), it was certainly not later on.

The principal form of local government therefore remained the manorial Court Leet, held twice yearly, which elected a High and Low Bailiff, two Constables and a Headborough, High and Low Tasters (aka Ale Conners and Flesh Conners) and, confirming the importance of the leather trade in mediaeval Birmingham, Searchers and Sealers of Leather. The Court met at the Manor House until the 1530s, then at the Leather Hall, then in the upper room of the High Cross (rebuilt 1703).

From the Tudor period, the Civil Parish took over many of the duties formerly carried out by religious gilds such as Birmingham's Gild of the Holy Cross (1392-1547), principally relief of the poor and maintenance of highways. The Parish officers, who met regularly in the Vestry) consisted of Churchwardens, Overseers of the Poor and Surveyors of the Highways (assisted by Scavengers). Although the Constables were elected at the Court Leet, they counted and were paid as Parish officers.

Another Tudor creation was the system of Justices of the Peace (aka Magistrates), who tended to be country gentlemen (Thomas Holte being a famous 17th century example) and of a Tory persuasion (as in the Priestley Riots). Equally unhelpful, for the most part, were the two Warwick County MPs, who provided the growing town with its sole voice in Parliament. From 1695, direct petitioning of Parliament by "the chief inhabitants and tradesmen" proved a more effective tool.

A first abortive attempt to get Birmingham incorporated was made in 1716 but many continued to hold the view, as expressed later in the century by William Hutton, that "a town without a charter is a town without a shackle". Any incipient demand that there may have been for parliamentary reform was quieted from 1774 to 1796 when one of the Warwick County MPs was always a "Birmingham" man. The only "public" buildings in Birmingham in the mid 18th century were the High Cross (1703), the Welsh Cross (1706), the prison in Pinfold Street (1733) and the Workhouse in Lichfield Street (1734). The first step to modernisation came with the creation of the Court of Requests (handling minor civil cases, especially debts) in 1752. Next came the Board of Guardians of 1783, which took over administration of the Poor Law. Most important of all was the establishment of Street Commissioners by the Improvement Act of 1769. Subsequent acts in 1773, 1801 and 1812 extended their powers and transferred many manorial and parish responsibilities.

The Street Commissioners were essentially an oligarchy of the wealthiest ratepayers but they played a major part in giving Birmingham the infrastructure it needed to become a great city. After decades of wrangling with the Manor, they finally acquired the all-important market rights in 1824. These had already been held on lease for a number of years, during which time the Bull Ring was cleared, street markets abolished and the new Smithfield

Market built on the site of the Manorial moat.

Having given Birmingham its first true public building in the shape of the Public Offices of 1807, the Street Commissioners reached their zenith in the 1830s with the building of the Market Hall and Town Hall.

But by this time moves were once more afoot to get Birmingham proper Parliamentary representation and proper local government. The man who became the leader of this campaign, Thomas Attwood, had the unusual background of being a banker and a Tory. More ironic still, his first emergence into public life was as manorial High Bailiff in 1812, petitioning Parliament for repeal of the 1807 Orders in Council, which were so damaging to Birmingham's trade.

Thomas Attwood, commemorated by this statue in Chamberlain Square, led the campaign to get Birmingham proper representation in Parliament

The classical Town Hall, begun in 1832, set the standard for civic buildings in Birmingham

Initial moves for parliamentary reform in 1817-19 were quashed but re-emerged ten years later. In 1830 Attwood formed the Birmingham Political Union, a "union of classes", which inspired a nation-wide push for reform. Mass meetings on Newhall Hill culminating with a 200,000 strong gathering on 7 May 1832 helped secure passage of the Reform Act. Birmingham finally became a parliamentary constituency, returning two MPs - not surprisingly, the first were Attwood and his deputy, Joshua Scholefield.

In 1835 the reformed Parliament passed the Municipal Corporations Act, doing away with mediaeval charters and allowing the new manufacturing towns to be incorporated. Birmingham petitioned for this in October 1837 and the Charter was granted on 1 November 1838. The first elected Council, comprising 48 members, was entirely composed of Liberals, although they had been opposed in every seat. Having failed at the ballot box, the Tories were far more successful at mounting a legal challenge to the Charter, leaving the Council virtually powerless until 1842.

The new borough had the same bounds as the 1832 parliamentary constituency, comprising not only Birmingham but also Edgbaston, Deritend & Bordesley and Duddeston & Nechells. This was the start of growth through annexation.

The old institutions hung on for a few more years: the Street Commissioners were abolished in 1851 and the last Court Leet held and High Bailiff elected in 1854. At long last Birmingham was beginning to function like the great town it was.

Victorian Birmingham 1 - the Dark before the Dawn

The Borough of Birmingham came into existence at the very start of the long reign of Queen Victoria. Its history in that period very much reflects the two sides of Victorian England - the grandeur and glory of an Imperial nation starkly contrasting with the "Dickensian" world of workhouse, poverty and social injustice.

For Birmingham the "glory" years came in the 1870s under the leadership of Joseph Chamberlain, but there had been plenty of "hard times" before.

Nationally, the 1840s was a decade of great advances in social legislation. A series of Acts of Parliament enabled Councils to create civic amenities in the shape of public baths, parks, recreation grounds, libraries, museums and art galleries. But Birmingham was slow to respond.

At first the Council was hampered by the division of responsibilities between itself and the Street Commissioners, who still controlled roads and drainage. But the sum total of its achievements in the first ten years after confirmation of the Charter in 1842 was one set of public baths (Kent Street 1851) and the Borough Gaol (1849) and Asylum (1850) which, together with the Board of Guardians' new Workhouse (1852), formed a sorry trio of institutions in Winson Green.

The Commissioners, meanwhile, were continuing to show the way. John Pigott Smith, appointed Surveyor in 1838, masterminded a scheme of road improvement, which won praise from the Institute of Civil Engineers in 1847, and began the mammoth task of creating a sewerage system in 1845 - his precisely surveyed maps at a scale of ten inches to the mile are a precious source for local historians. Almost by accident, the Commissioners also found themselves

The Western Road approach to the Birmingham
Workhouse in Winson Green, one of a sorry trio of
institutions established there in the 1840s and 50s

involved in Birmingham's first slum clearance schemes when they approved the sites for New Street and Snow Hill railway stations, the former in the notorious Froggery district.

However, criticism of them in the Rawlinson Report that followed the Public Health Act of 1848 eventually led to their powers being handed over to the Council under the Improvement Act of 1851.

The Council, its resources trebled overnight, now had no excuse not to undertake the already overdue provision of public amenities. But it was at this very moment that a split emerged in its ranks between factions who became known as the "extravagants" (who wanted to spend money on improvements) and the "economists" (who wanted above all to keep the rates down). The latter became dominant under the leadership of butcher's son, Joe Allday.

The situation may seem surprising in a Council dominated by Liberals, but it must be remembered that the electorate, which at this stage comprised only 3% of the population, was predominantly made up of small businessmen, and the Council reflected this with 55% of its membership from the same group.

As the town's principal ratepayers, they had a vested interest in low rates, and were strong supporters of the "laissez-faire" economic thinking of the time. It is interesting to note that Rawlinson's report not only criticised the appalling health conditions in the courts of back-to-back housing but also pointed out bad sanitation in Edgbaston where the problem was not lack of money but an unwillingness to spend it.

Frustrated at every turn, the Council's Public Works and Finance committees resigned en masse in 1855, leaving Allday's men to take over. Two years later Pigott Smith was removed, his drainage scheme left in virtual abeyance. In an age when Medical Officers were seen as essential in most big towns, Birmingham's half-time equivalent was dismissed as surplus to requirements. The only two positive steps taken were the purchase of land near the Town Hall for a future civic centre and the opening of Calthorpe Park (leased at a very low rental from Lord Calthorpe) in 1857.

The tide began to turn in 1858 with the visit of Queen Victoria to open Aston Hall and Park (a private venture at this stage). A new sense of civic pride temporarily swung the balance against the "economists" and cost them their leader, who left the Council in 1859. The 1861 Improvement Act was forced through despite severe opposition and a few public projects undertaken: the drainage scheme was revived with, after 1865, the establishment of sewage farms along the Tame; new public baths were built in Woodcock Street, Gosta Green (1860) and Northwood Street, Hockley (1862); the first municipal cemetery was opened at Witton in 1863; Adderley Park was finally taken over by the Council in 1863, having been originally offered by the owner in 1854 and opened privately in 1856; Aston Hall and Park were acquired in 1864.

A growing tide in favour of social reform was further signalled when the provisions of the 1850 Free Libraries Act were finally adopted locally in 1860, leading to the opening of the first branch library in 1861 and the Central Reference Library in 1866.

The speech given at the opening ceremony by non-conformist preacher, George Dawson outlined his "Civic Gospel", that a town should be run like a church in which the poorer members of the community are cared for by the better off. The same message was coming from the Congregationalist, Dale, the Baptist, Vince and the Unitarian, Crosskey.

A light in the darkness - Deritend Free Library in Heath Mill Lane is the sole survivor of the new libraries of the 1860s which heralded a new age of social reform

There were laymen too who heard the message. In 1867 George Dixon and Jesse Collings formed the Birmingham Education Society which, through its creation of the National Education League in 1869 contributed immensely to the 1870 Education Act. One of its younger members was a London-born businessman who had arrived in Birmingham in the 1850s and, like so many other Unitarians, Quakers and other non-conformists, recognised a responsibility to play a role in local society. In 1869 he was elected to the Council and rapidly became the figurehead of the progressives, who were now almost ready to take on the "economists" once and for all. The showdown came in the November elections of 1873 when their champion stood against "economist" candidate, James Brinsley, a local grocer. The result was a landslide and Joseph Chamberlain became Mayor of Birmingham.

Victorian Birmingham 2 -
the Best Governed City

"The history of nineteenth-century Birmingham, particularly the Birmingham of Chamberlain, is so closely bound up with the history of England as a whole, that a local history of the city is an essential chapter in the history of the nation." (Asa Briggs)

When Joseph Chamberlain was elected Mayor of Birmingham in 1873 he predicted, "In twelve months by God's help the town shall not know itself". The call upon the deity came straight from the heart, but Chamberlain, like the Unitarian creed to which he belonged, was more concerned with this world than the next.

The reforms he initiated led to Birmingham being dubbed "The Best-Governed City in the World" by American, J. Ralph in an 1890 magazine article, in which he observed, "Birmingham is above all else a business city, run by business men on business principles". Religion may have been the inspiration but pragmatism was the means.

It was pragmatism that dictated that gas rather than water should be the first of the long delayed "municipalisations" to take place. The idea that municipalities could run their own gas works had been around since 1817 and by 1870 there were 33 such undertakings. The necessary powers for Birmingham to do the same had been included in the 1861 Improvement Act but had lain dormant until now.

Chamberlain saw ownership of the highly profitable gas concern as the means to generate funds for other projects. The take-over in 1875 was so successful that within seven years profits of almost £200,000 had been made, allowing gas prices to be lowered by a third and borough rates to be reduced. Gas profits also financed building of the Museum and Art Gallery above the department's

*The Chamberlain Memorial Fountain in Chamberlain Square honours
the man who made Birmingham "the best governed city in the world"*

offices - the motto on the memorial stone reads, "By the gains of Industry we promote Art".

Water was a different matter - as Chamberlain said, "the power of life and death should not be in the hands of a commercial company, but should be conducted by the representatives of the people". The powers for "municipalising" water dated back even farther than those for gas - to the 1851 Improvement Act - but they were only finally used in 1875.

Two other measures date to this incredible year in Birmingham history: the setting up of a Health Committee to support the work of the Medical Officer who had ultimately been forced on the borough by the 1872 Public Health Act; and the utilisation of the slum clearance powers granted by the Artisans' Dwellings Act to clear the way for the creation of Corporation Street.

As with all the other Chamberlain measures, the development of Corporation Street was vigorously opposed by local Tories, who were satirised as opposing simply because "it was a Chamberlain scheme, and must, therefore, be vile and ruinous and pernicious and wicked and against the constitution and the scriptures". Begun in 1878, progress was intermittent with the final stretch beyond Lancaster Street (making the whole thing almost a mile long) only approved in 1903. The ambitious enterprise finally became a profit-maker in the 1930s.

Chamberlain was more justly criticised by his enemies for his failure to follow up the building of his "Parisian boulevard" with the creation of new housing to replace the cleared slums. The omission was partly justified by a housing report in 1885 that showed no shortage, but the problem returned to haunt the city in the 20th century. In 1913 there were still 200,000 Brummies living in 43,366 back-to-backs, compared with 2,881 in Liverpool and none in Manchester.

The first corporation housing, established in Ryder Street and Lawrence Street from 1889 was only a partial answer, as were the improved back-to-backs known as "Nettlefold Courts" (after the chair of the Housing Committee, which came into existence in 1901).

Chamberlain's election as mayor had come in the same year as another Liberal election victory - this time to take control of the School Board established by the 1870 Act. The first new Board School was opened in Bloomsbury in March 1873, with 28 more by 1880. It was later said, "In Birmingham you may generally recognise a Board School by its being the best building in the neighbourhood. In London it is almost a case of vice versa". The first secondary school was opened in Waverley Road in 1892. Birmingham also made provision for higher education, establishing the country's first municipal School of Art in 1885.

The Chamberlain reforms, which also included the creation of a borough Fire Brigade in 1874, were considerably assisted by his party's total dominance at both local and national elections. The "caucus" system of tactical voting won all three Birmingham parliamentary seats from 1867 to 1885 and all seven of the new seats at the first election thereafter. But the "Liberal schism" of 1886, prompted by Chamberlain's resignation from the government (which he had joined after leaving local politics and becoming an MP) on the issue of Irish Home Rule let in the Conservatives. Ultimately the Liberal Unionists and the Conservatives were to unite, locally in 1919.

The struggles of Birmingham industry to cope with the new competition from Germany and the USA, which had so badly devastated the Black Country, eventually led Chamberlain to abandon his free trade principles and promote tariff reform, with dire consequences for the Conservative/Unionist government of 1906.

Birmingham continued to reach new heights in the 1880s and 1890s: the Birmingham Corporation Consolidation Act in 1883; the grant of Assizes in 1884 (Queen Victoria laid the foundation stone of the new Law Courts in 1887); County Borough status in 1888; City status in 1889; Lord Mayoralty in 1896; "municipalisation" of electricity in 1899; and, most important of all, the League and Cup Double for Aston Villa in 1897!

The remarkable achievements of the 1870s must, it is true, be seen in the context of a national economic boom in 1870-73 that was so good that the government was at one stage considering the abolition of income tax (!), and, at the same time, with due awareness of how far Birmingham had fallen behind other towns in the 1850s and 60s - but it was still an epoch-making time when Birmingham set standards which were emulated and aspired to all over the world.

Oozells Street Board School of 1877, now the Ikon Gallery, one of dozens of high-quality schools built in Birmingham following the 1870 Education Act

Twentieth Century Birmingham 1 - Greater Birmingham

The twentieth century opened with Birmingham continuing to develop along the lines laid down by Joseph Chamberlain. The University, chartered in 1900 and with its new Edgbaston campus inaugurated by Edward VII in 1909, was largely his initiative and had him as its first Chancellor. The long-term ambition to see Birmingham's water supply assured was finally achieved in 1904 with the opening, again by Edward VII, of the 73-mile aqueduct from the Elan Valley in Wales to the new reservoirs at Bartley Green.

The University of Birmingham, chartered in 1900 had its Edgbaston campus inaugurated by King Edward VII in 1909

A further mark of Birmingham's coming of age was the creation of its own Anglican diocese in 1905, with St Philip's elevated to a cathedral.

The Chamberlain belief in municipal ownership continued with the take-over by the city of the tramways in 1903. Horse-drawn trams had been running since the 1870s and there had been experiments with steam, cable and battery trams until the electric wire tram arrived in 1901. The Corporation acquired its first omnibuses in 1913.

Major changes were in the air in Birmingham industry. The workshop based craft industries that had made Birmingham great in the 18th century were finally giving way to mechanisation and mass production, a process that culminated during the First World War. Electrical engineering and motor car manufacture were to be the dominant industries of the twentieth century.

The trend to establish massive new factories on green field sites went back to BSA at Small Heath in 1861 and, most famously, Cadbury's relocation to Bournville in 1879. Major new plants established in the early years of the new century include GEC at Witton, Fort Dunlop in Erdington and Austin's at Longbridge.

Herbert Austin was neither Birmingham's only nor first motor pioneer. While he was still working for the "Wolseley Sheep Shearing Machine Company" in Broad Street, Frederick William Lanchester was designing Britain's first four-wheel, petrol-driven car in 1895. Lanchester, Wolseley and Austin all became famous names.

The spread of new factories and the growth of public transport was opening up more and more of the surrounding area to the Birmingham workforce. The most forward-looking scheme for accommodating these new "commuters" was the vision of George Cadbury, who created Bournville Village in the 1890s and handed it over to its own Trust in 1900. The emphasis on quality building and green space provided a model for the "garden cities" of later years. This encroachment of Birmingham into its neighbours also led to calls for the creation of a "Greater Birmingham" incorporating all

*A replica of Britain's first real motor car, designed
by F W Lanchester, unveiled in Bloomsbury Park
during the Lanchester Centenary Rally in 1995*

the districts now dependent on the city. The first "annexations" had
been made in 1891 with Harborne (Staffordshire), Balsall Heath
(Worcestershire) and Saltley and Ward End (Warwickshire)
becoming parts of Birmingham. Following a period in the 1890s
and early 1900s when Birmingham Council seemed to be losing
some of its drive, the old zeal was re-ignited by the accession of
Quinton in 1909 and "Greater Birmingham" became a crusade.
There was strong resistance from neighbouring county councils
(after all, Handsworth by itself was bigger than Oxford and
represented a tenth of the rateable value of the whole county) but
eventually deals were struck and in 1911 Aston and Erdington
(Warwickshire), Kings Norton, Northfield and Yardley
(Worcestershire) and Handsworth (Staffordshire) joined the city,
giving it a total population of around 850,000 and confirming it
without doubt as the nation's Second City.

The massive expansion of city services brought new demands. One of the men who stepped forward to answer them was Joseph Chamberlain's son, Neville, Lord Mayor in 1915-16. His greatest local initiative, earning him a call up to national government, was a municipal scheme arguably more revolutionary than anything his father had done. Begun as a short-term wartime measure to promote savings, the controversial "Birmingham Corporation Savings Bank" was so successful that it was re-founded in 1919 as the Birmingham Municipal Bank, opening the way to savings and mortgages to hundreds of thousands of ordinary Brummies.

Birmingham was of course a vital part of the war effort in 1914-18. Despite the huge number of men - and increasing numbers of women - engaged in industry, the city still sent 150,000 of its people to fight, of whom 35,000 came back disabled and 13,000 did not come back at all. The three largely abortive Zeppellin raids on the city in 1916, 1917 and 1918 were a portent of future horrors.

The 1920s and 30s saw a great building boom to accommodate the city's ever-growing population - over 100,000 new houses were built, roughly half by the Corporation and half by private enterprise. Some of the new estates were so big that they were small towns in themselves - Kingstanding estate was bigger than Shrewsbury. At first, the new estates lacked any facilities, making inhabitants dependent on public transport - fortunately this was also the time when tram and, increasingly, bus services were reaching their peak, the new Outer Circle bus route of 1926 pointing the way towards a tram-less future.

For all the great building projects in the suburbs, the old, old problem of inner-city slum-land continued, with 38,773 back-to-backs still remaining in 1935. Ambitious plans for an enormous new Civic Centre in Broad Street were left unrealised, but the city did enter the age of air travel with the opening of Elmdon Airport in 1939.

Through all this time, following the death of Joseph Chamberlain in 1914, Neville and his older brother, Austen had continued to represent Birmingham's interests in Parliament. Neville almost lost his Ladywood seat to Labour in 1924, the year of Birmingham's first Labour MP, but went on to be Chancellor of the Exchequer and ultimately Prime Minister. As Chancellor, in 1933, he formally opened Birmingham's 40,000th council house in Weoley Castle. Little surprise, then, that as Prime Minister, later in the decade, he did all he could to avert the war that was to do so much damage to his beloved city. Universally vilified and hounded from office, he died on November 9, 1940, just days before Coventry and then Birmingham were subjected to the worst the Luftwaffe could throw at them.

Twentieth Century Birmingham 2 - Forward!

Between August 1940 and April 1943 Birmingham was hit by more high explosives than any British city other than London and Liverpool/Birkenhead. In strict terms of economics, the 65 air-raids had little real effect, knocking only a few percent off production levels. But, in human terms, the cost was far greater with 2,241 people killed and some 3,000 seriously injured.

The first big raid was on August 25/26, 1940 when the city centre was targeted and the Market Hall gutted. After the "coventration" of Coventry on November 14/15, Birmingham was attacked by 350 bombers on November 19/20 - with more casualties than in any other raid, including fifty workers at BSA - and again by 200 aircraft on November 22/23, when damage to the water supply left the city dangerously vulnerable to a follow-up raid - which fortunately never came. The longest raid, lasting thirteen hours, was on December 11/12 (St Thomas' church destroyed) but there were no more big raids until 9/10 April 1941 (1,121 casualties, "Big Top" area blitzed) and only sporadic incidents thereafter.

In some ways, the Luftwaffe didn't do enough - although some 12,000 houses were damaged, a third of them beyond repair, a post-war report showed 51,000 sub-standard homes in need of demolition, many in the long-neglected inner city slum areas. The problem took over 30 years to solve, and in many cases the measures taken proved deeply unpopular.

More than ever after the war, Birmingham was no longer its own master. Government legislation dictated what could be done and government subsidies became an ever more vital part of local finances. Municipal institutions such as gas, water, electricity and public transport were either regionalised or nationalised.

There was also a change in Birmingham's own government, with

St Thomas' Peace Garden in Bath Row remembers the past and looks to the future in the shadow of a church destroyed by bombing in 1940

the last "patrician" councillors dying out to be replaced by career politicians. National party politics impinged more and more on local elections - Conservatives in the Council ceased to call themselves Unionists in the 1950s. But Birmingham politics retained its own identity, with both parties generally more moderate than the national bodies. The old split between "economists" (usually Conservative) and "extravagants" (usually Labour) re-emerged, assisted by a shift towards "individualism" and away from "the common good" among the electorate.

It was in this new political climate that the rebuilding of Birmingham took place. Hampered by post-war government spending restrictions, the city was unable to address immediately its housing problems and had to resort to erecting thousands of temporary "pre-fabs" (some of which saw in the Millennium still occupied). When building finally began in earnest in the 1950s, the deficit was so great that the Council had to abandon its "low density" principles and put up the hated high-rise blocks.

The housing situation was worsened by a government-imposed end to the "Greater Birmingham" dream of perpetual expansion. "Green Belt" land around the city was jealously guarded, while neighbouring boroughs, many of whose residents were better-off people who had moved out of Birmingham, fought hard against annexation. The one exception to this was the incorporation of Sutton Coldfield in the city in 1974, but Solihull's successful preservation of independence was more typical.

One solution to Birmingham's plight was the creation of satellite towns at some distance away in the 1960s: "new towns" at Telford and Redditch and a town development scheme at Daventry. The 1970s saw Birmingham itself becoming part of something bigger - West Midlands County - but the experiment was short-lived.

Redevelopment of the city centre was stimulated by construction of the Inner Ring Road or Queensway between 1957 and 1971. Sadly, it also destroyed many historic buildings, leading to the birth of the local conservation movement, which arrived on the scene just in time to save Colmore Row.

Centenary Square, with its high-class hotels and
International Convention Centre, has become
the symbol of the new Birmingham

A major change in the make-up of Birmingham's population resulted from mass immigration after the war. By 1991 around 20% of the population came from ethnic minorities, with some districts topping 50%. Race relations in the city have generally been better than in other places, with the Handsworth riots of 1985 the lowest ebb.

Birmingham's Irish community also had its problems, particularly following the IRA pub bombings of 1974. Nor did the local police emerge very well from the enquiry that led to the release of the alleged bombers, the "Birmingham Six", in 1991.

Birmingham industry continued to be dominated by the manufacturing sector, but it was this that suffered worst in the recessions of the 1970s and 80s, when over 100,000 jobs were lost. Many famous names in manufacturing went to the wall, while others lost their independence to multi-national concerns.

Revival came in the shape of increased reliance on service industries. Beginning with the National Exhibition Centre (1976), Birmingham has since invested in other major facilities such as the International Convention Centre (1991) and the National Indoor Arena. In keeping with the city's new international image, Elmdon Airport was considerably expanded and renamed Birmingham International in 1984. And, just as with the canals of the 18th century and railways of the 19th, Birmingham is at the heart of the 20th century's most important transport network - the motorways.

The many new initiatives taken by a once more bullish City Council led to it being dubbed "the inheritors of Chamberlain" in a 1991 *Financial Times* article. But for Chamberlainite values, things had come full circle in the 1980s with the privatisation of utilities and the former Municipal Bank (merged with TSB 1976).

The 21st century begins with the Bull Ring still at the heart of things, as it has been since at least the 12th century. The concrete blocks that replaced the ancient street market in the early 1960s are now themselves being replaced in a new large-scale redevelopment for the Millennium.

What happens next is up to you!

Further Reading

Bassett, S   2000   Anglo-Saxon Birmingham, *Midland History,*
                            XXV, 1-27

Briggs, A   1952   *A History of Birmingham Volume II: Borough
                            and City 1865-1938*, OUP

Chinn, C   1994   *Birmingham: The Great Working City*,
                            Birmingham City Council

Chinn, C   1996   *Brum Undaunted: Birmingham During the Blitz*,
                            Birmingham City Council

Chinn, C   1999   *One Thousand Years of Brum*, Birmingham
                            Evening Mail

Gill, C   1952   *A History of Birmingham Volume I: Manor and
                            Borough to 1865*, OUP

Holt, R   1985   *The Early History of the Town of Birmingham
                            1166 to 1600 (Dugdale Society Occasional
                            Papers No. 30)*

Hopkins, E   1998   *The Rise of the Manufacturing Town:
                            Birmingham and the Industrial Revolution*,
                            Sutton (Revised Edition of *Birmingham: The
                            First Manufacturing Town in the World, 1760-
                            1840*, Weidenfeld & Nicolson, 1989)

Hutton W   1783   *An History of Birmingham* (1976 Reprint with
                            introduction by C.R. Elrington), EP Publishing

Skipp, V   1979   *The Centre of England*, Methuen

Skipp, V   1980   *A History of Greater Birmingham - down to
                            1830*, (New Edition 1997), Brewin Books

Skipp, V   1983   *The Making of Victorian Birmingham*
                         (New Edition 1996), Brewin Books

Stephens, WB   1964   *A History of the County of Warwick Volume*
                         VII:The City of Birmingham (Victoria History of
                         the Counties of England), OUP

Sutcliffe, A   1974   *A History of Birmingham Volume III:*
& Smith, R   *Birmingham 1939-1970*, OUP

Upton, C   1997   *A History of Birmingham* (Revised Edition),
                         Phillimore